Canada's D-Day Heroes

ON JUNO BEACH

Introduction by **J. L. Granatstein** Text by **Hugh Brewster**

A Scholastic / Madison Press Book

The Courage of Canadians

On Juno Beach today, dogs play in the surf and sunbathers spread their blankets. This part of France's Normandy coast is popular with vacationers. But sometimes other visitors come here. They're old men, often wearing berets or blue blazers decorated with medals. Some of them are in wheelchairs, pushed by their wives or one of their children or grandchildren. And they're always Canadian.

They come here to remember what happened on this beach sixty years ago, on June 6, 1944 – a day called D-Day. They were young then, many of them only teenagers. But in the face of fierce enemy gunfire, they struggled ashore to help free France from the tyranny of Adolf Hitler. D-Day was one of the great decisive battles in all of history. If the Allied forces of the United States, Great Britain and Canada had been driven back into the sea by the Germans, the Second World War might have been lost. Certainly, the casualties would have been terrible, and France and much of Europe would have remained enslaved by the Nazis for years. But the D-Day invasion succeeded; the liberation of Europe was underway – and with it, the beginning of the end of World War II.

Colourful war posters (above) were designed to boost the morale of Canadians during World War II. (Opposite) Chaplain Robert Seaborne of the Canadian Scottish Regiment leads men in prayer as they cross the English Channel to Juno Beach on June 6, 1944.

"They were young then, many of them only teenagers. But in the face of fierce enemy gunfire, they struggled ashore to help free France from the tyranny of Adolf Hitler."

(Left) Canadian prime minister Mackenzie King, left, U.S. president Franklin Roosevelt, centre, and British prime minister Winston Churchill meet at Quebec in August of 1943 to discuss the invasion of France.

1944
1944
YEAR OF DECISION
"The supreme effort has still to be made".
Rt. Hon. W. L. Mackenzie King

(Above) Tanks stand ready for shipment to Europe at a war plant in Montreal. (Right) A sixteen-year-old female rivet catcher waves from her post at a Pictou, Nova Scotia, shipyard. Women joined the workforce in record numbers during the war. (Bottom left) A boy runs after his father as he marches off to war from New Westminster, B.C. (Inset) Large arrows in a 1944 war poster target Nazi-occupied Europe.

When Adolf Hitler's Nazi Germany invaded Poland on September 1, 1939, most Canadians believed that his aggression had to be stopped. But Canada's armed forces numbered only 10,000 men and they had little modern equipment – no tanks, no aircraft and just a handful of ships. Only five years later, by the spring of 1944, Canada's navy was on the way to becoming the third largest in the world, its air force the fourth biggest. From a population of 11 million people, 1.1 million men and women served their country in uniform.

So when D-Day came, the Canadians were ready. The 3rd Canadian Division was the assault force; its men came from all across Canada, serving in regiments with proud names such as the Royal Winnipeg Rifles, *Le Régiment de la Chaudière* and the North Shore (New Brunswick) Regiment. These soldiers crossed the English Channel on ships of the Royal Canadian Navy, while overhead the Royal Canadian Air Force provided cover in Lancaster bombers and Spitfire fighters. By nightfall on June 6, 1944, Canada's forces had gone further inland than any other Allied army. Before the Normandy campaign was over, 5,000 young Canadians would give their lives and 18,000 more would be wounded in body and mind. A band of brothers? Absolutely.

Today, Canadians scarcely remember D-Day.

Almost no Canadians – except, perhaps, your great-grandfathers and great-grandmothers – remember that Canada provided one-fifth of the attacking force and that the navy and air force played a huge role on D-Day and afterwards. How many Canadians even know that the Second World War was about great questions of freedom and the survival of democracy?

It is important not to forget such things. Canadians today live in a prosperous, democratic and free nation because our ancestors fought to protect their country – and the world – from the monstrous evil that Nazi Germany and its allies represented. Few recall that our then-small country played so important a role in building the tanks and trucks and producing the food and raw materials on which Allied victory depended. The Canadians of the Second World War years were not all heroes in the front line, but many of them were. They risked everything, and the 42,000 who did not return to Canada gave their todays for our tomorrows.

It matters that we remember those who fought. We can still talk to some of the now-old men and women who won the Second World War. They deserve our thanks for their courage, for giving up their youth to serve their nation's greatest interests. They deserve Canada's gratitude – and yours.

– *J. L. Granatstein*

WESTERN EUROPE: SPRING 1944

Allied-controlled

Axis-controlled

Neutral country

German prewar border

NORWAY

SWEDEN

UNITED
KINGDOM

North
Sea

DENMARK

NORTHERN
IRELAND

ATLANTIC WALL

IRELAND

EAST PRUSSIA
(GERMANY)

ENGLAND

Pas de Calais

NETHERLANDS

Berlin

London

POLAND

NORMANDY
INVASION
BEACHES

English Channel

BELGIUM

Dieppe

GERMANY

Paris

CZECHOSLOVAKIA

FRANCE

SWITZERLAND

AUSTRIA

HUNGARY

SPAIN

ITALY

YUGOSLAVIA

Rome

ALBANIA

Mediterranean Sea

GREECE

SICILY

NORTH AFRICA

Hitler's "Fortress Europe"

In the spring of 1944, Europe was still firmly in the grasp of Adolf Hitler. But after five years of war, the tide was beginning to turn against him. Allied forces, including 60,000 Canadians, were fighting their way up the boot of Italy. Russian troops were advancing from the east. In England, two million troops were training for a massive invasion of Nazi-occupied France. Hitler knew that an Allied invasion was coming and he had built an "Atlantic Wall" – fortifications that ran from Norway down along the coast of France. The heaviest defences were near the Pas de Calais, the shortest route across the English Channel. Hitler was sure that that was where the Allies would invade. But Supreme Allied Commander Dwight Eisenhower and his advisors had another plan. The beaches of Normandy were a good place to land boats and men. And since this coast was not as well defended, the Allies might be able to take the enemy by surprise. Above all, the Allied commanders wanted to avoid a disaster like the one that had occurred almost two years before, on the beach in front of a town called Dieppe.

(Above) Field Marshal Erwin Rommel, centre, and German soldiers look out to sea from one of the thousands of concrete bunkers along the French coastline. Hitler had made Rommel responsible for repelling an Allied invasion in France. (Left) This German gun battery still stands on the Normandy coast.

"Everything indicates that the enemy will launch an offensive against the Western front of Europe, at the latest in the spring…."

— Adolf Hitler, November 1943

7

The Tragic Lesson of Dieppe

On the night of August 19, 1942, an Allied force of 6,100 men – 4,963 of them Canadians – crouched in landing craft off the French coast. Their orders were to launch a raid at dawn on the Nazi-held port of Dieppe. But everything went wrong: the Germans were on the alert and gunned down the troops as they scrambled ashore. Most of the Allied soldiers never even made it off the beaches. In all, 907 Canadians were killed, 586 were wounded and 1,946 (including many wounded) were taken prisoner. The raid has been called "the bloodiest nine hours in Canadian military history."

"I said to myself, 'Well, Lucien, old bean, this is where you finish your life, in the dirty waters of Dieppe.'"

— Sergeant Lucien Dumais, *Les Fusiliers Mont-Royal*

(Opposite) Canadian troops are shelled as they storm ashore at Dieppe, as depicted by war artist Charles Comfort. Most of the tanks (top) got stuck among the baseball-sized pebbles of the beach. Bodies and wrecked equipment (above) lie on the beach after the raid. (Right) Surviving Canadians are marched off to a German prisoner-of-war camp.

Over Before It Began

Sergeant Lucien Dumais,
Les Fusiliers Mont-Royal

"One of the Germans was yelling at me, but I could not understand him. Then he gestured to me to throw down the rifle and raise my hands. I took the handkerchief from the bayonet and threw the rifle down onto the shingle [pebble] beach. The bayonet dug itself in and the rifle stuck, butt end up, the way we mark the spot where a soldier lies wounded or dead.... Resignedly, I raised my hands above my head...."

Planning Operation Overlord

"An operation the nature and size of Operation Overlord has never previously been attempted in history."

— from the offical outline of the planning document for D-Day

The Allies learned valuable lessons from Dieppe – though at a high cost. When the time came to invade Nazi-occupied France, they would be prepared. The plans for Operation Overlord, as the invasion was code-named, were over two years in the making. From an elegant mansion in the south of England, General Eisenhower and his commanders plotted the route of the mightiest invasion force ever assembled. Five thousand ships were to carry 130,000 men and 20,000 vehicles, supported by 700 warships and 8,000 aircraft. All these were to converge along an 80-kilometre stretch of the Normandy coast. Five beaches had been selected for the landings and given code names. Omaha and Utah were to be taken by the Americans; Sword and Gold were for the British. One beach, called Juno, was to be attacked by Canadians.

The D in D-Day

D-Day is a general military term for the day a planned attack will take place. The "D" doesn't stand for anything. There have been many D-Days in history – though June 6, 1944, is the most famous.

(Above) The helmet worn by Canadian soldiers on D-Day is sometimes called an "invasion helmet." Beside it is a copy of the secret plan, carried by every Allied unit, describing its place of landing and specific mission. (Left) Canada's troops were commanded by General H.D.G. "Harry" Crerar, standing. His boss was General Sir Bernard "Monty" Montgomery, left, commander-in-chief of the invasion, who in turn reported to the supreme Allied commander, General Dwight D. "Ike" Eisenhower, right.

ENGLAND

Felixstowe

Harwich

Sheerness

London

Southwick House
(Invasion Headquarters)

Southampton

Portsmouth

Weymouth

Poole

Newhaven

Portland

ENGLISH CHANNEL

Dartmouth

American Airborne Assault

British and Canadian Airborne Assault

Cherbourg

Dieppe

UTAH   OMAHA   GOLD   JUNO   SWORD

Le Havre

Seine River

Caen

FRANCE

(Left) The routes from ports on England's south coast to the targeted Normandy beaches. (Below) Royal Canadian Navy commandos during training exercises in preparation for D-Day.

Mulberries, Funnies & Phonies

From Dieppe, the Allies had learned that seizing a defended enemy port was too difficult. But without a harbour, how could they land all the heavy equipment and supplies they would need for an invasion? The solution was to create enormous floating concrete docks – code-named "Mulberries" – that could be ferried across the English Channel after the initial D-Day attack and then sunk to create temporary ports where ships could unload.

(Left) A Mulberry artificial harbour under construction in April 1944. Labouring in secret, 25,000 workers built 213 massive concrete sections for two harbours in seven months. Each of the 6,000-tonne Mulberry sections was then towed across to France and placed on top of sunken ships (below) known as "Gooseberries." (Bottom) The remains of a Mulberry harbour can still be seen off the town of Arromanches today.

Ingenious new tanks were also invented. Known as "Hobart's funnies" (after their inventor, Major-General Percy Hobart, and their unusual appearance), some featured cannons that would blast out sea walls and bunkers; others boasted revolving drums covered in chains to blow up mines. The most common "funny" was the DD (duplex-drive) tank. Nicknamed "Donald Duck" by the troops, the DD had waterproof canvas sides and propellers to drive it through the water. Once it was on the beach it could drop its sides and fight like a normal tank.

And some tanks were completely fake. To keep the Germans from guessing the actual location and date of the invasion, phantom armies with phony tanks, jeeps and ships were created. From the air, the dummy equipment looked real and enemy spy planes were fooled into thinking that troops were massing at other locations instead of England's south coast.

(Above, right) A DD tank enters the water with its canvas sides up and (bottom) advances on land with its sides collapsed. (Above, centre) A Sherman Crab tank uses its revolving drum with chains attached to sweep for mines. (Inset) This vehicle laid a roadway for the tanks that followed behind it. (Above, left) A dummy tank made of wood and canvas. (Opposite, top) Fake shoulder patches for two phantom airborne divisions.

Waiting for D-Day

*"The worst part of any action is waiting.
We all wanted to get on with it."*

— Craftsman Arthur Wildman,
Royal Canadian Electrical and Mechanical Engineers

By the spring of 1944, the thousands of Canadians in England had been training for many months. The armies had carried out massive drills in landing craft and on beaches. Paratroopers had performed hundreds of practice drops. At the end of May, the soldiers were sent to camps in the south of England. There they were completely sealed off from the public — no letters or telephone calls could be sent or received. On June 1, the first Canadians began boarding the ships that would take them across to Normandy. The fifth of June was the target date for the invasion, but the weather was causing treacherous squalls in the English Channel. On June 4, General Eisenhower met with his admirals and generals — and the weatherman. The forecast suggested that the bad weather might lift for twenty-four hours on June 6; conditions would not be favourable again for weeks. The final decision was Eisenhower's, and thousands of lives depended on it. In the early hours of June 5 he announced, "Okay, we'll go."

(Opposite, left) Soldiers of the Queen's Own Rifles of Canada at a D-Day training camp in England. After many months of exercises, such as training on obstacle courses (opposite, top right), the Canadians were more than ready for D-Day to begin. (Opposite, bottom right) The Queen and Princess Elizabeth visit the paratroopers of the 1st Canadian Parachute Battalion. (Above) During a practice run, men of the Highland Light Infantry of Canada board one of the landing craft that will take them to Normandy.

Parachuting into France

"The jump went well for me but not so for many of my comrades, who found themselves in flooded marshes and drowned there...."

— Private Roger Charbonneau, 6th Airborne Division

Shortly after midnight on June 6, 1944, as the people of Normandy slept, paratroopers from the 1st Canadian Parachute Battalion jumped out of planes into the cold, dark night. They had an important job to do: the 156,000 soldiers from Canada, Britain and the United States who were on their way across the English Channel were depending on the paratroopers to destroy bridges and gun batteries before the big invasion. It was a cloudy, windy night with no moonlight. When the paratroopers landed, they were scattered over a large area. Many of them were miles from their targets. Others landed successfully in their drop zones, found their comrades and completed their missions.

(Opposite, left) These snapshots show practice jumping during the weeks before the invasion. (Opposite, right) Dummy decoys called "Ruperts" were dropped along with the real paratroopers on June 6, 1944. (Above) Members of the 1st Canadian Parachute Battalion jump from planes during training exercises for D-Day.

Alone in a Strange Place

Private Jan de Vries,
1st Canadian
Parachute Battalion

"As I made my way, I tried to figure out what went wrong; why I was alone in a place where I could not recognize any features we had studied in the transit camp. Just before daylight I met three men from my platoon…. We continued together and finally arrived late in the day at our high ground defence position…. Out of the 120 men in C Company who were to carry out the objectives, only 35 landed in the drop zone. The rest were scattered like myself or captured or killed. Some straggled in for days if they had managed to evade the Germans…. The four of us cursed the pilot who had dropped us so far away when we were told of the battles that had taken place."

The Eyes of the Army

Flight Lieutenant James B. Prendergast, 430 Squadron,
39 Reconnaissance Wing, Royal Canadian Air Force

"Our wing was selected to be the 'eyes' of the 2nd British Army. Overnight our aircraft had been partially repainted with black and white stripes to reduce confusion with German planes, many of which had similar silhouettes.... Crossing over the Channel at dawn on June 6, we were overwhelmed by the flotilla of different boats and landing craft en route to Normandy. An incredible sight! We were given specific instructions from General Montgomery to advise immediately on the status of the control of the Pegasus Bridge. The British and Canadian armies, arriving overnight by glider and parachute, were to capture the bridge from the Germans. At 7:30 A.M. there were still some firefights taking place between the Germans and our troops near the bridge. Flying at about 200 feet [60 metres] I could identify the troops by their helmets and saw that our team had control of the bridge, with the Germans slowly retreating in the distance...."

The Flyers

During April and May of 1944, the Royal Canadian Air Force had been bombing roads, bridges, railways and command centres in Normandy – and in the Pas de Calais area, to make it seem as though that was the area targeted for invasion. In the early days of June, RCAF Lancaster bombers dropped thousands of tonnes of explosives on the concrete bunkers and gun emplacements of Hitler's Atlantic Wall. Then, under cloudy skies on June 6, Canadian fighter pilots battled the German *Luftwaffe* (air force) in aerial dogfights as they tried to protect the soldiers on the beach below.

James Prendergast (above) made three flights over Normandy on D-Day in his P-51 Mustang airplane, nick-named *Lazy Lady*. On one mission he spotted a German armoured division that the Allies hadn't known about.

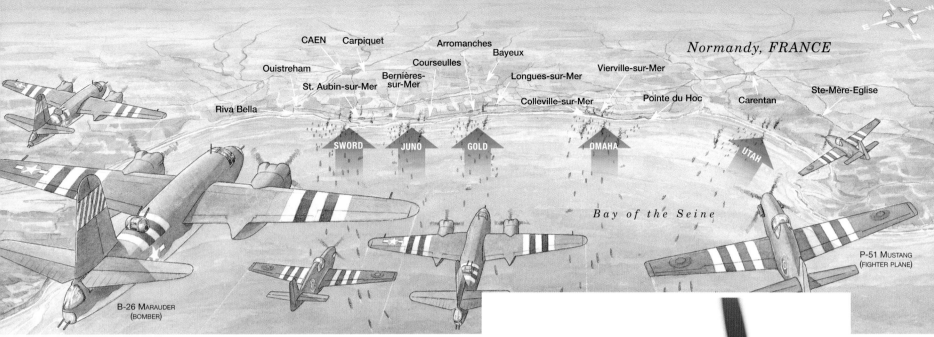

Normandy, FRANCE

CAEN Carpiquet Arromanches Bayeux

Ouistreham Courseulles Vierville-sur-Mer

St. Aubin-sur-Mer Bernières-sur-Mer Longues-sur-Mer Ste-Mère-Eglise

Riva Bella Colleville-sur-Mer Pointe du Hoc Carentan

SWORD JUNO GOLD OMAHA UTAH

Bay of the Seine

P-51 MUSTANG
(FIGHTER PLANE)

B-26 MARAUDER
(BOMBER)

(Above) Hundreds of Canadian airmen flew as part of the 171 Allied squadrons that attacked on D-Day. During the fighting in Normandy, the RCAF bombed and strafed German divisions. (Right) A Canadian pilot climbs into his Hawker Typhoon fighter-bomber. Nicknamed the "Tiffy," the Typhoon carried eight rocket missiles under its wings that were a key weapon for destroying German tanks. (Bottom right) Two RCAF armourers load ammunition for the Typhoon's small-calibre cannons. (Below) Tinted flying goggles improved a pilot's vision during night flights.

19

The Greatest Armada

"…the greatest armada ever created by man. Compared with this, the Spanish sailed against England with a two-bit fishing fleet."

— Cliff Bowering, soldier and writer

(Below) At dusk on June 5, thousands of ships prepare to sail across to Normandy. The barrage balloons overhead helped protect them from enemy airplanes. (Inset) This tattered flag was rescued from a sunken Canadian landing craft off Juno Beach.

In the chilly darkness before dawn on June 6, the mightiest invasion force in history began cutting its way through the waters off the coast of England. An armada of 5,000 ships, carrying 130,000 men, was accompanied by 700 warships —

including six monstrous battleships. Sixteen Canadian minesweepers helped clear the path as 126 ships and 10,000 sailors of the Royal Canadian Navy carried Canadian troops into battle.

(Right) On board one of the troop transport ships, Company Sergeant-Major D. D. Perkins of Ottawa writes a letter home. Other soldiers (inset) played cards to pass the time. (Above) Packed into a landing craft, Canadian troops head toward Juno Beach.

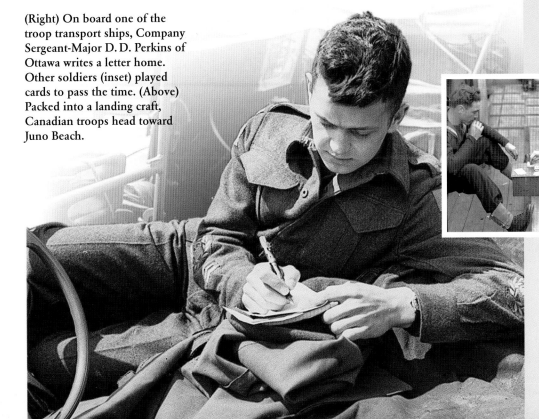

EYEWITNESS

Lance-Corporal William Bleackley, 1st Battalion, Canadian Scottish Regiment

"The feeling, for me at least, was more intense during the approach to the beach than on the beach itself…whether you're going to come back, whether you're going to return to a normal life, or whether my life would be snuffed out."

EYEWITNESS

George Lynch-Staunton, 14th Field Regiment, Royal Canadian Artillery

"Most of us were below decks. And most of us, other than when we were being fed, because there was really nothing else to do, other than to look at our maps, most of us played cards. Some played poker, some played bridge, whatever."

EYEWITNESS

"Brother, this is for real." Cliff Bowering, soldier and writer

"You're in the water now. In the breakers. You try to remember how to walk in the water and keep your rifle up and dry. Yard by yard you move in. Smoke up ahead, and the noise…it's like nothing you've ever heard before, even in the blitz in England. What a difference between this and battle camp. Brother, this is for real."

Attack on Juno Beach

"We were told not to stop and help any of our buddies as we too might be hit."

— Wilfred Bennett, Royal Winnipeg Rifles

As the soldiers headed toward the beach in their landing craft, they were surrounded by explosions and gunshots. Behind them, hundreds of ships blasted shells at the German guns on the shoreline. Above them, the fighter pilots dropped bombs and fired at targets. The sea was rough and many of the men were violently sick as their landing craft tossed and rocked in the two-metre-high waves. When the soldiers arrived at the shore, underwater mines ripped apart landing vessels around them, throwing many of them into the cold water. Shivering and wet, the men crawled onto the beach amid machine-gun fire.

(Above, left) A Royal Canadian Navy landing craft heads for the beach. (Above, right) Canadian troops prepare to leave their landing craft. (Inset) Canadians at home awoke to D-Day headlines. (Opposite) Troops come ashore at Juno Beach, in this painting by war artist Orville Fisher.

"We're on the beach to stay."

Many of the troops who landed in the first wave on Juno Beach faced heavy gunfire, but the Queen's Own Rifles of Toronto took more punishment than any other regiment. The tanks that were supposed to land ahead of the Queen's Own came late, enabling German machine gunners to mow down the soldiers as they raced for the

"I was the eleventh off."

Lance-Corporal Rolph Jackson, Queen's Own Rifles of Canada

"We got fairly close to the beach; the water didn't even come up to our hips. Slightly on our right was a German pillbox [gun emplacement]. It was manned. There were about thirty men on our landing craft. I was the eleventh off. Eight of those first eleven were killed and two of us were wounded. I was hit in the hand. It must have caught me off stride because it knocked me down. The front of my pants and my battledress blouse were shredded. Farther up the beach I tangled with a grenade thrower. The potato masher [German grenade] landed in front of me. I hit the ground and picked up a fragment in my shoulder. I got to my feet, tossed a grenade over the [sea] wall. It burst before it hit the ground. Fortunately, something had already blown a large hole in the wall and we went through it."

(Above) Rolph Jackson, and (right) a shoulder flash and cap badge of the Queen's Own Rifles of Canada.

"We've got the strength and support. We're on the beach to stay. We've landed in France. We're on our way!"

— Cliff Bowering

sea wall. One hundred and forty-three of the unit's men died on the beach. But by the afternoon of D-Day, most of the German defences had been smashed and Canadian forces had moved into some of the coastal towns. The roads leading from Juno Beach were crowded with tanks and troops and littered with the debris of war.

(Opposite and right) Men of the Stormont, Dundas and Glengarry Highlanders, carrying bicycles like the one at left, come ashore in the second assault wave. The bikes proved hard to ride and were soon abandoned.

The End of the Longest Day

"It had been and always will be the longest day."
— Rifleman Jim Williams, Queen's Own Rifles of Canada

"That very first night," Private Angus Kearns of the 1st Battalion, Canadian Scottish Regiment, remembered, "we started burying our dead. When you start burying your buddies, you think, what's the use in going on? But we did."

By the end of D-Day, 340 Canadians had given their lives, 574 were wounded and 47 had been taken prisoner. But one troop of Canadians from Ontario's 1st Hussars had pushed further inland than any other Allied unit. In all, the Allies landed 130,000 troops by sea and 23,000 by air on D-Day, along with several thousand vehicles and tonnes of supplies. Hitler's Atlantic Wall had been breached – but the battle had just begun.

(Opposite, top left) Army medics treat a wounded soldier during the first assault wave. They would have used a canvas bag for bandages, like the one shown at right. (Opposite, bottom) Wounded soldiers lie beside the sea wall at Bernières-sur-Mer. (Left) Later on June 6, German prisoners of war wait to be shipped to England. (Above) Lieutenant William McCormick, centre, and his troop from the 1st Hussars went the furthest inland on D-Day.

"I was there to take photographs. But you can't put the smell into the photograph…the awful smell of death. That's when you realize war is not a game…not fun." — Captain Ken Bell,
Canadian Army Film Unit

"Je suis Canadien."

The people in the towns near Juno Beach were overjoyed to be liberated.

"That's my home over there, ruined," one French girl said. "But the Allies are here!" A man from the village of Courseulles-sur-Mer saw the men in khaki on the beach and said to one in English, "Here they are, the Tommies [English soldiers]!" The young man answered in French: *Je suis Canadien.* The men of Le Régiment de la Chaudière – or *Chauds,* as they were known – were given a particularly warm welcome. Centuries before, some of their ancestors had sailed from Normandy. On hearing the Norman pronunciation used by one Chaud, a French villager kissed the soldier on both cheeks and said, "You're not a Canadian, you're a Frenchman like me!"

(Left) A Canadian medic treats the burned leg of a French boy while his brother looks on. (Centre) Citizens of Bernières-sur-Mer wheel away possessions from their wrecked homes. (Right) A World War I veteran greets the liberators with a French flag. (Opposite) Two Norman children play soldiers with a helmet, like the one shown above, and an old Canadian officer's hat.

Moving Inland

In the days after D-Day, the goal for the Canadians was to capture the city of Caen. But on the road to Caen, the Germans were ready and waiting for them. Near the village of Authie, the men of the North Nova Scotia Highlanders and the Sherbrooke Fusiliers ran into the elite 12th SS Panzer Division. Under the command of a hardened veteran, *Brigadeführer* (Colonel) Kurt Meyer, the teenagers of the 12th SS were ferociously loyal to Hitler.

They fought savagely, and the big guns on their tanks torched many of the Canadian tanks, forcing a retreat. Meyer ordered that twenty-three captured Canadians be shot, then had some of the bodies thrown onto the road. Soon other Canadian regiments arrived on the battlefield and slowly pushed the Germans back. But after six days, more than 1,000 Canadians had died, nearly 2,000 were wounded – and Caen was still in German hands.

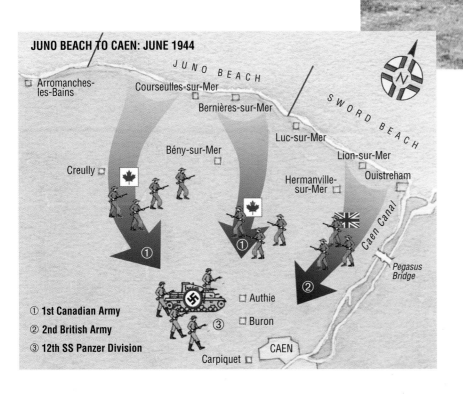

JUNO BEACH TO CAEN: JUNE 1944

Arromanches-les-Bains
Courseulles-sur-Mer
Bernières-sur-Mer
JUNO BEACH
SWORD BEACH
Luc-sur-Mer
Bény-sur-Mer
Lion-sur-Mer
Creully
Hermanville-sur-Mer
Ouistreham
Caen Canal
Pegasus Bridge
①
②
Authie
Buron
③
① 1st Canadian Army
② 2nd British Army
③ 12th SS Panzer Division
Carpiquet
CAEN

(Opposite) On the way to Caen, infantrymen walk as tanks rumble by. At night they rested in slit trenches (inset, bottom) and sometimes scrounged meat (inset, top) to supplement their canned rations. The Canadians' Sherman tanks (above) were no match for the superior tanks of the 12th SS Panzer Division. Troops of the 12th SS, led by Kurt Meyer (right), were responsible for killing 156 captured Canadians in Normandy. Meyer was tried for war crimes in 1945, and served eleven years in prison.

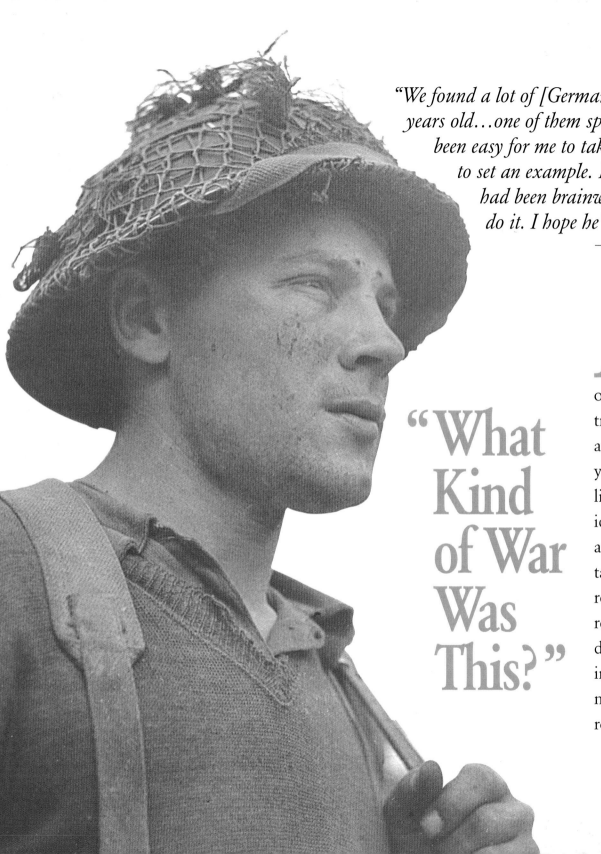

"We found a lot of [German] teenagers, fifteen or sixteen years old…one of them spat in my face…. It would have been easy for me to take my .38 revolver and shoot him, to set an example. But I did not. He was young, he had been brainwashed. Today I'm proud I did not do it. I hope he's still alive today."

— Major Michel Gauvin, *Le Régiment de la Chaudière*

"What Kind of War Was This?"

Although many of the Canadians who fought in Normandy were only in their late teens, the German soldiers were often even younger. With the German troops stretched thinly across Europe, and reinforcements scarce, soldiers as young as fifteen were sent to the front lines. All had been educated in Nazi ideals in the Hitler Youth organization and were angry and defiant when taken prisoner. Their comrades who remained to fight put up ferocious resistance to the Canadians in the drive for Caen. Throughout June and into July the fighting continued, and more Canadians died, yet Caen remained in German hands.

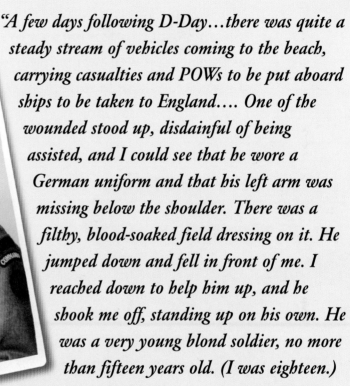

"He was no more than fifteen…"

William K. Newell, W Commando,
Royal Canadian Navy

"A few days following D-Day…there was quite a steady stream of vehicles coming to the beach, carrying casualties and POWs to be put aboard ships to be taken to England…. One of the wounded stood up, disdainful of being assisted, and I could see that he wore a German uniform and that his left arm was missing below the shoulder. There was a filthy, blood-soaked field dressing on it. He jumped down and fell in front of me. I reached down to help him up, and he shook me off, standing up on his own. He was a very young blond soldier, no more than fifteen years old. (I was eighteen.) He stood very close to me, staring into my eyes. Then he spat in my face, and turned and walked up the ship's ramp. My emotion turned in a flash from one of sympathy to one I couldn't name, and my first impulse was to shoot him. Lowering my weapon, I just stood there shaking my head…. What kind of a war was this?"

(Opposite) The strain of battle shows on the face of Private Harry Parker of the Highland Light Infantry. (Above) A sullen and defiant teenage soldier from the 12th SS is taken prisoner. Other young German prisoners (below) wait to be interrogated. (Right) William K. "Bill" Newell in his naval commando's uniform.

Tending the Wounded

"It seemed to be a help to have a woman there."

— Jean Ellis, Canadian Red Cross Nurse

With so many soldiers being wounded in the fight for Caen, nurses were desperately needed. In July, the first Canadian nurses arrived, ready to work and live in the tents of the field hospitals. "I was assigned a row of twenty-five beds," remembers Jean Ellis. "Parts of uniforms had to be cut off, and I was so afraid of hurting the men…I shook like a leaf. Many of the patients were delirious and kept calling out 'Mother…' all day long."

The Penicillin Queen

Nora Cook, Nursing
Sister, #10 Canadian
General Hospital

"There was mud everywhere...and no water to wash sheets.... Doctors worked around the clock and we did, too.... The sad part was seeing all those young chaps without arms and legs.... There were infections of all kinds.... Penicillin had just been developed...and was not available in Canada yet.... I went up and down and shot everyone with penicillin. That's how I got my name — I was called the Penicillin Queen."

(Opposite) Nurses with the #10 Canadian General Hospital, Royal Canadian Army Medical Corps, land at Arromanches on July 23, 1944. (Right) A jeep serving as an ambulance races through a Norman town. Although nurses worked long, hard hours in the field hospitals, the army preferred to release photographs of them doing more "feminine" tasks, such as looking at a soldier's arm cast (inset, top) or folding bandages (inset, bottom).

"A Shocking Rubble Heap"

General Montgomery and the other Allied commanders had decided that Caen had to be captured at any cost. On the night of July 7, waves of British bombers dropped tonnes of explosives. But when the Canadians entered the ruined city, they found that almost all the Germans had escaped to the city's outskirts. Instead, the bombing had killed hundreds of citizens of Caen and wounded thousands more.

(Right) Canadians enter the heavily bombed Carpiquet Airfield on the outskirts of Caen, in this painting by Orville Fisher. (Left) In a ruined church in Carpiquet, a soldier pauses before a statue of the Virgin Mary. (Above, left) British heavy bombers pound Caen on July 7, 1944. (Above, right) Canadian artillery guns fire on the city in preparation for the infantry attack.

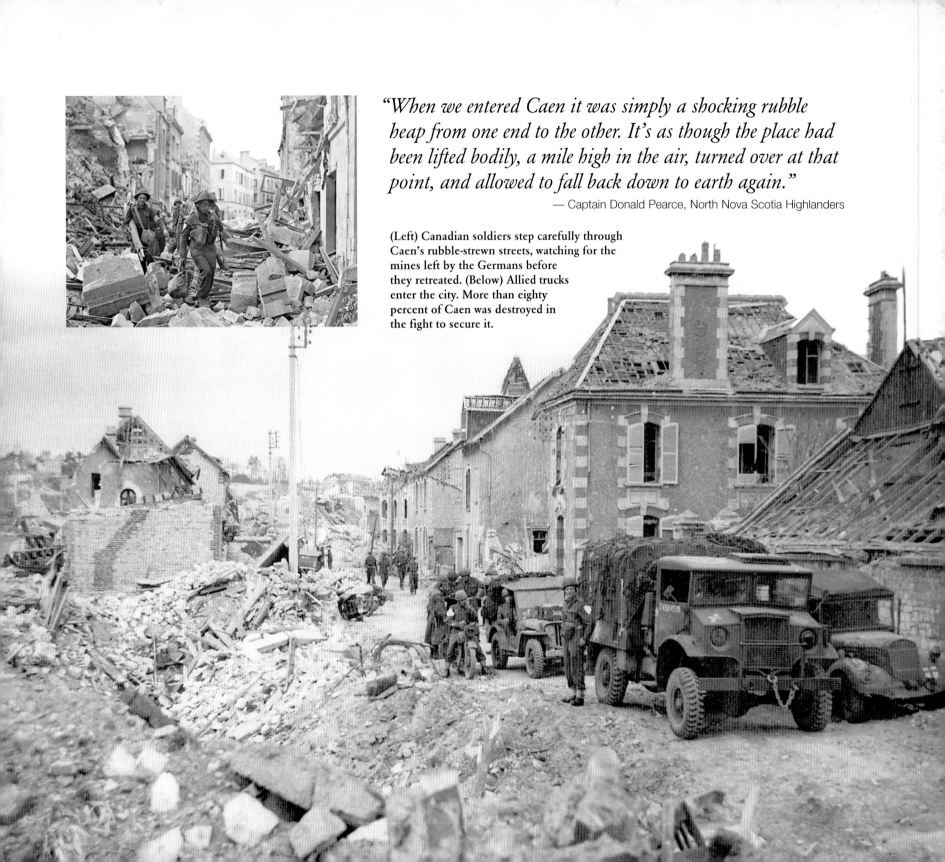

"When we entered Caen it was simply a shocking rubble heap from one end to the other. It's as though the place had been lifted bodily, a mile high in the air, turned over at that point, and allowed to fall back down to earth again."

— Captain Donald Pearce, North Nova Scotia Highlanders

(Left) Canadian soldiers step carefully through Caen's rubble-strewn streets, watching for the mines left by the Germans before they retreated. (Below) Allied trucks enter the city. More than eighty percent of Caen was destroyed in the fight to secure it.

Earned in Blood

"All day and all night, the guns, blasting the way for the fighting men. Millions of shells helping to win this close, bloody and ferocious battle in Normandy...."

— Matthew Halton, reporting for CBC Radio

After Caen, the Canadians were ordered to fight their way south into open country. But each mile would be earned in blood. On July 25, Montreal's Black Watch Regiment made a brave charge up a ridge near the village of Verrières – and 123 of them never returned. In all, more than

450 Canadians would die that day – after Dieppe, it was the bloodiest day of the war for Canada. But with the cream of the German army fighting the Canadians and the British near Caen, the American forces were able to break through the enemy defences to the west. The Germans were now in trouble. They should have retreated and regrouped behind the River Seine, but Hitler would not hear of a retreat. The Allies quickly saw their chance. They would trap and defeat the Germans near a town called Falaise.

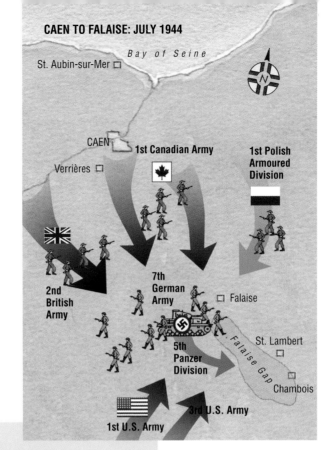

CAEN TO FALAISE: JULY 1944

Bay of Seine

St. Aubin-sur-Mer

CAEN

Verrières

1st Canadian Army

1st Polish Armoured Division

2nd British Army

7th German Army

Falaise

5th Panzer Division

Falaise Gap

St. Lambert

Chambois

1st U.S. Army

3rd U.S. Army

South of Caen, the Canadians suffered many casualties. On July 25, Montreal's Black Watch Regiment (badge shown, opposite, top) lost 123 men. (Below) Chaplain Robert Seaborne prays for a dying soldier. (Opposite, left) Two Canadians take turns firing through a loophole in the wall of a former French barracks. (Opposite, bottom right) Canadian and British tanks head south toward Falaise.

EYEWITNESS

"We buried him in an orchard."

Sergeant M. Brimble

"My dear Mr. and Mrs. Duncan: It is with my deepest regret that I have to write you a letter of this nature…. Your son was my Platoon Commander… and met with an accident which proved fatal…. I can say this with great pride, that he will always be remembered by his boys and myself…. We buried him in an orchard…in as good a grave as is permitted under these conditions…. I must close now with the regret of the whole platoon and myself on your sad bereavement. Yours, M. Brimble"

The Road to Falaise

The Allied plan called for the Canadian, British and Polish forces to advance on Falaise from Caen and link up with the Americans approaching from the south. But enemy resistance on the road to Falaise was fierce, making for a long and gruesome struggle. In early August, as the Allies closed in, some of Hitler's troops were escaping through a small area called the Falaise Gap. And it was up to the Canadians to seal the opening. On August 18 the last open road in the gap ran through the village of St. Lambert-sur-Dives. There, a small band of men from the South Alberta Regiment and the Argyll and Sutherland Highlanders, led by Major David Currie, overcame a huge German force. They destroyed 7 enemy tanks, 40 vehicles and took 2,100 German prisoners. It was a heroic finish to a brutal and bloody campaign. The toll for the Germans was terrible — more than 10,000 were killed, 60,000 wounded and 40,000 taken prisoner. But with the closing of the Falaise Gap, the Allies had finally overtaken the Germans in Normandy.

"We went into the Falaise Gap at Chambois...and saw absolute carnage...."
— British Sergeant-Major Laurence Symes, fighting with the Canadians

"We just streamed back...."

German paratrooper Gerhard R. Käppner

"We couldn't take any of our equipment...we just streamed back with our small arms.... If we weren't attacked we just kept quiet and moved out during the night.... We got back as far as Belgium...by surprise, we got caught by mortar fire...something hit me on the head and some on the face, and that was the end of the war for me."

(Opposite) Canadian soldiers walk past a burning tank on the road to Falaise. The climax of the battle for the Falaise Gap came on August 18 in the town of St. Lambert-sur-Dives when German soldiers (above) surrendered to Canadians under the command of Major David Currie, third from left. Currie was awarded the Victoria Cross (inset), the British Commonwealth's highest decoration for gallantry, for his actions that day. (Right) Gerhard Käppner's German army identification.

41

Victory

"Pianos lined the streets, as many as fifty per street in some districts; and again all played the same music for street dancing."

— Captain Donald Pearce, North Nova Scotia Highlanders, in London, England, on V-E Day

What the Canadians achieved at Falaise helped lead to the liberation of Paris on August 25, 1944. An even more meaningful date for Canadians was September 3, when men from the regiments that had fought in the Dieppe raid marched through a freed Dieppe to honour their comrades who had died there. Canadians went on to liberate the Netherlands in April of 1945. On May 1, Hitler committed suicide. The war ended on May 7, 1945, when Germany surrendered. The next day, May 8, was declared V-E Day, which stood for Victory in Europe. Giant parties were held all over Europe, Canada and the United States. Now the Canadian men and women who had spent years away from their

(Left) Toronto's *Evening Telegram* headlined news of the German surrender on May 7, 1945. The next day, V-E Day celebrations took place in the streets of Toronto (above) and in many other cities.

families could finally return home. They were happy that the war was over, but some were also nervous about returning to everyday life. Living through the war had changed them. They had witnessed unspeakable horrors and had seen many of their friends die. Would they want to return to the lives they had lived before? How much had changed while they were away?

(Right) Returning Canadian soldiers crowd the decks of their troopship as it enters Halifax harbour. (Below) On September 3, 1944, the men of the 2nd Canadian Division march through a liberated Dieppe to a simple cemetery that the townspeople had made for the Canadians who had died there two years before.

Arriving Home in Canada

Jean Ellis, Canadian Red Cross Nurse

"Closer and closer we sailed…. Necks were craned to catch a first glimpse of Halifax. Tears flowed down many cheeks…. Suddenly, Halifax harbour fireboats appeared, shooting off huge sprays of water as a welcome to the thousands of Canadian boys and girls who had risked their lives and futures for their country's safety. The band on the docks started up, and 'O Canada' sounded sweeter than ever before."

Our Finest Day

"Coming back here, going to the cemetery, you can't stop the tears from flowing."

— Frank Ryan, North Shore (New Brunswick) Regiment

Every year on June 6, Canadian veterans return to Juno Beach. And every year there are fewer of them. It will not be very long before there are only gravestones and memorials left to remind us of the men who risked and sacrificed their lives in this greatest of all invasions. To keep the stories of these brave men alive for future generations, Canadians from all across the country contributed money to help build the Juno Beach Centre in the town of Courseulles-sur-Mer. This museum opened on June 6, 2003.

Closer to home, some D-Day veterans, most of them well into their eighties, regularly make visits to schools. They tell students about what happened that day, about the friends they lost, and why all Canadians, young and old, should remember.

(Opposite) Flowers bloom amid the graves at the Canadian War Cemetery at Bény-sur-Mer, recalling the poppies (above) that Canadians wear on Remembrance Day. Canada lost 9,900 soldiers in Normandy, the highest per capita sacrifice of any Allied nation. (Right) Veteran Jan de Vries (see page 17) salutes at a ceremony honouring D-Day paratroopers on June 6, 2003.

GLOSSARY

Allies: the nations – including Canada, the United States, Britain and the Soviet Union – that fought against Germany and its partners during World War II.

armada: a large group of warships.

armourers: soldiers responsible for the upkeep of guns and other small arms.

artillery: weapons such as large guns and cannons.

Axis: the nations – including Germany, Italy and Japan – that fought against the **Allies** in World War II.

barrage balloons: blimps, anchored to the ground or attached to ships with cables, that prevent low-flying enemy planes from passing through.

bayonet: a sharp steel blade attached to the end of a rifle.

breakers: waves that break into foam, especially when striking the shore.

bunker: a structure, built of concrete and often dug into the earth, that provides shelter from attacks.

calibre: the size of ammunition a firearm carries. The calibre is usually determined by the diameter of either the bullet or the weapon's barrel.

casualties: soldiers who are killed, injured or captured during battle.

flotilla: a small group of boats or ships.

gun battery/emplacement: a defensive position from which weapons are fired.

Hitler Youth: a government organization that educated German children in **Nazi** ideals. Boys were trained as soldiers and girls were prepared for motherhood.

infantry: soldiers on foot.

medic: an unarmed soldier whose duty is to give medical care to the wounded on a battlefield.

minesweeper: a ship that clears away floating and underwater mines.

Nazi: a member of the political party headed by Adolf Hitler. The Nazis' central belief was that the German people and culture were superior to those of other races and cultures.

panzer: a German word for armour. World War II German tanks were called panzers, and armoured units were known as panzer divisions.

penicillin: a medicine that prevents the growth of certain germs that cause disease.

POW: prisoner of war.

reconnaissance: a military survey of enemy territory.

regiment: an army unit, usually commanded by a colonel, that is made up of smaller groups called companies, squadrons or batteries.

reinforcements: soldiers and supplies sent to strengthen an army.

SS: the *Schutzstaffel*. An elite group of the **Nazi** party that guarded Adolf Hitler, fought as **infantry** and armoured units in battle, and acted as security forces in German-controlled countries.

sea wall: a wall built to protect a beach from being washed away.

shells: explosive rounds fired by **artillery**.

Tommies: a nickname for British soldiers.

INDEX

PICTURE CREDITS

All maps are by Jack McMaster.
C/M – CORBIS/Magmaphoto.com
CWM – Canadian War Museum
IWM – Imperial War Museum
MUL – Canadian War Poster Collection,
 Rare Books and Special Collections
 Division, McGill University Libraries
NAC – National Archives of Canada
NARA – National Archives and Records
 Administration
QORC – Queen's Own Rifles of Canada
 Regimental Museum
WKN – Courtesy of William K. Newell

Front cover: WKN. (Inset, top) MUL. (Inset,
 bottom left) NAC PA-122765. (Inset,
 bottom right) QORC.
Back cover: (Top to bottom) Courtesy of
 William McCormick. QORC. Courtesy of
 James B. Prendergast. WKN. NAC PA-
 136280.
2: MUL.
3: NAC PA-129054.

4: (Top left) NAC C-2450. (Inset, left) MUL.
 (Bottom left) NAC C-038723. (Inset, right)
 NAC WRM 1799. (Right) NAC WRM 2515.
6: (Left) Hulton-Deutsch Collection/C/M.
7: (Left) Peter Christopher. (Right) AKG London.
8: CWM.
9: (Top) NAC C-029878. (Middle) NAC
 C-014160. (Bottom) NAC C-014171.
10: (Left) NAC PA-136327. (Right) QORC.
11: (Bottom) WKN.
12: (Top) U.S. Army Quartermaster
 Museum, Fort Lee, VA. (Bottom left) Naval
 Historical Center. (Bottom right) IWM
 BU1036.
13: (Top left) The National Archives, Surrey,
 United Kingdom. (Top middle, top right
 and inset) The Tank Museum. (Bottom)
 NARA.
14: (Top) QORC.
 (Bottom right, above) NAC PA-132776.
 (Bottom right, below) NAC PA-129047.
15: NAC PA-132811.
16: (Left) Courtesy of Eric Sykes. (Right)
 Jackson Hill/National D-Day Museum.
17: (Left) Strathy Smith/NAC PA-132785.
 (Right) Courtesy of Jan de Vries.
18: Courtesy of James B. Prendergast.

19: (Left) Canada Aviation Museum.
 (Right, inset) NAC PL-40736. (Bottom right)
 NAC PL-30936.
20: NARA. (Inset) WKN.
21: (Top left) Bettmann/C/M. (Bottom left)
 NAC PA-132881. (Inset) NAC PA-132794.
22: CWM.
23: (Left) Dennis Sullivan/NAC PA-132790.
 (Right) IWM FLM3566. (Inset) Courtesy of
 Gary Pawson.
24: (Top) G. A. Milne/NAC PA-122765.
 (Bottom) D-Day Museum.
25: (Top) QORC. (Bottom) CWM.
26: (Left) Frank L. Dubervill/NAC
 PA-136280. (Right) Courtesy of William
 McCormick.
27: (Top left) NAC PA-36697. (Top right)
 Canada Science and Technology Museum,
 photo by Helen Graves-Smith. (Bottom)
 Frank L. Dubervill/NAC PA-132384.
28: (Top) QORC. (Bottom left) NAC
 PA-141703. (Bottom middle) NAC PA-
 132725. (Bottom right) NAC PA-131386.
29: Ken Bell/NAC PA-132724.
30: NAC PA-132846. (Inset top) NAC
 PA-132885. (Inset bottom) NAC PA-129039.
31: (Top right) NAC PA-132801. (Bottom
 right) Ullstein Bilderdienst.

32: NAC PA-131401.
33: (Top) NAC PA-114495. (Middle) WKN.
 (Bottom) NAC PA-132872.
34: Harold G. Aikman/NAC PA-108174.
35: (Left) Ken Bell/NAC PA-129031. (Top
 right) Ken Bell/NAC PA-131427. (Bottom
 right) NAC PA-131389.
36: (Left) Ken Bell/NAC PA-116545. (Inset)
 IWM CL347. (Top right) Ken Bell/NAC
 PA-116516. (Bottom right) CWM.
37: (Left) Hulton-Deutsch Collection/C/M. (Inset)
 IWM B6799.
38: (Left) NAC PA-132852. (Top right)
 Courtesy of Captain Andrew Kerr.
 (Bottom right) NAC PA-116525.
39: (Bottom right) NAC PA-137537.
40: Ken Bell/NAC PA-131375.
41: (Top left) Donald I. Grant/NAC PA-
 111565. (Inset) Courtesy of David
 Handley. (Bottom right) Second World
 War Experience Centre.
42: (Left) Toronto Public Library. (Right)
 NAC PA-114626.
43: (Right) York University Archives. (Inset)
 NAC PA-131323.
44: Peter Christopher.
45: (Left) Royal Canadian Legion. (Right)
 WO Jean Blouin, DND-CF.

QUOTATION CREDITS

Ken Bell, William Bleackley, *Canada Remembers: Part One, Turning the Tide: 1939 to D-Day*, National Film Board of Canada, 1995.

Wilfred Bennett, *Voices of D-Day: The Story of the Allied Invasion Told by Those Who Were There*, edited by Ronald J. Drez, Louisiana State University Press, 1994.

Cliff Bowering, *Legion Magazine*, excerpted in *A Terrible Beauty: The Art of Canada at War*, edited by Heather Robertson, James Lorimer & Co., 1977.

M. Brimble, *Some Letters and Other Writings of Donald Albert Duncan*, Imperial Publishing, 1954.

Michel Gauvin, Nora Cook, *Canada Remembers: Part Two, The Liberators: D-Day to the Rhine*, National Film Board of Canada, 1995.

Lucien Dumais, *The Man Who Went Back*, Leo Cooper, 1975.

Jean Ellis, *Face Powder and Gun Powder*, S. J. R. Saunders, 1947.

Matthew Halton, *The Canadians at War: 1935/45, vol. 2*, Reader's Digest Association, 1969.

Gerhard Käppner, courtesy of the Second World War Experience Centre.

Angus Kearns, *The Canadians at War: 1935/45, vol. 2*, Reader's Digest Association, 1969.

George Lynch-Staunton, *D-Day Plus Fifty*, CBC, 1994.

Donald Pearce, *Journal of a War*, Macmillan, 1965.

Frank Ryan, *D-Day Plus Fifty*, CBC, 1994.

Laurence Symes, Imperial War Museum Sound Archives (13952/5, 1994).

Arthur Wildman, Imperial War Museum Sound Archives (9139/1 and 3, 1985).

Many thanks to Roger Charbonneau, Rolph Jackson, William K. Newell, Jim Prendergast and Jim Wilkins for sharing their memories with us.

Every effort has been made to clear copyright and correctly attribute all photographs and quotations. If any errors have unwittingly occurred, we will correct them in future editions.

SELECTED BIBLIOGRAPHY

BOOKS

Bell, Ken. *Not in Vain*. Toronto: University of Toronto Press, 1973.
–. *The Way We Were*. Toronto: University of Toronto Press, 1988.
Chandler, David G. and James Lawton Collins, Jr., eds. *The D-Day Encyclopedia*. New York: Helicon, 1994.
Collier, Richard. *D-Day: June 6, 1944 – The Normandy Landings*. New York: Abbeville Publishing Group, 1992.
Copp, Terry. *Fields of Fire: The Canadians in Normandy*. Toronto: University of Toronto Press, 2003.
Dumais, Lucien. *The Man Who Went Back*, London: Leo Cooper, 1975.
Ellis, Jean M. *Face Powder and Gun Powder*. Toronto: S. J. Reginald Saunders & Co., 1947.
English, John A. *The Canadian Army and the Normandy Campaign: A Study of Failure in High Command*. New York: Praeger, 1991.
Granatstein, J. L. *Normandy 1944: Canada Remembers*. Ottawa: Government of Canada Veterans Affairs, 1994.
Granatstein, J. L. and Desmond Morton. *Bloody Victory: Canadians and the D-Day Campaign 1944*. Toronto: Lester Publishing, 1994.
Hillsman, John Burwell. *Eleven Men and a Scalpel*. Winnipeg: The Columbia Press, 1948.
Oliver, Dean F. and Laura Brandon. *Canvas of War: Painting the Canadian Experience – 1914 to 1945*. Hull, Que.: Canadian Museum of Civilization Corporation; Vancouver/ Toronto: Douglas & McIntyre; Ottawa: Canadian War Museum, 2000.
Pearce, Donald. *Journal of a War*. Toronto: Macmillan, 1965.
Reader's Digest. *The Canadians at War: 1935/45, Vol. 2*. Montreal: Reader's Digest Association, 1969.
Robertson, Heather, ed. *A Terrible Beauty: The Art of Canada at War*. Toronto: James Lorimer & Company, 1977.
van der Vat, Dan. *D-Day: The Greatest Invasion – A People's History*. Vancouver: Raincoast Books, 2003.

VIDEOCASSETTES

Canada Remembers: Part One, Turning the Tide: 1939 to D-Day, prod. Kent Martin, dir. Terence Macartney-Filgate, 53 min. 40 sec., National Film Board of Canada, 1995.
Canada Remembers: Part Two, The Liberators: D-Day to the Rhine, prod. Kent Martin, dir. Terence Macartney-Filgate, 55 min. 19 sec., National Film Board of Canada, 1995.
D-Day Plus Fifty, prod. Ken Dodd and Eric Posner, 60 min., CBC, 1994.

WEBSITES

Several museums and organizations have websites with good information about Canadians in World War II. For addresses, simply use your search engine with the names shown below.

The Canadian War Museum
The Dominion Institute: The Memory Project
Maple Leaf Up: The Canadian Army Overseas

In addition, most of the Canadian regiments who fought at D-Day, such as *The Queen's Own Rifles* and *Le Régiment de la Chaudière* have their own websites.

ABOUT THE AUTHORS

Hugh Brewster won both the Silver Birch and Red Cedar Awards in 1998 for *Anastasia's Album: The Last Tsar's Youngest Daughter Tells Her Own Story*. He is also the author of *Inside the Titanic*, and co-author of *882 1/2 Amazing Answers to All Your Questions about the Titanic* and *To Be A Princess*.
J. L. Granatstein is the author of more than thirty books on Canadian history including *Bloody Victory: Canadians and the D-Day Campaign*, *The Good Fight: Canadians and World War II* and *Canada's Army: Waging War and Keeping the Peace*.

ACKNOWLEDGMENTS

The author and Madison Press Books would like to thank J. L. Granatstein for his eloquent introduction and expert advice. Thanks are also due to Dominic Farrell for photo research, and to Catherine Fraccaro, Ian Coutts, Dan Black of the Royal Canadian Legion and Sandy Bogart Johnston and Solange Champagne-Cowle of Scholastic Canada. Special thanks to the veterans and their families for sharing pictures and memories.

Introduction © 2004 J. L. Granatstein
Text, cover, design and compilation
© 2004 The Madison Press Limited

Madison Press Books
1000 Yonge Street, Suite 200
Toronto, Ontario
Canada M4W 2K2

National Library of Canada Cataloguing in Publication

Brewster, Hugh
 On Juno Beach : Canada's
 D-Day heroes / Hugh Brewster ;
 introduction, J.L. Granatstein.
 "A Scholastic/Madison Press Book".
 ISBN 0-439-96728-7
 1. World War, 1939-1945–
 Campaigns–France–Normandy–
 Juvenile literature. 2. Canada.
 Canadian Army–History–World War,
 1939-1945–Juvenile literature. I. Title.

 D756.5.N6B74 2004
 j940.54'21422   C2003-905166-8

 1 3 5 7 9 10 8 6 4 2

Editorial Director: Hugh Brewster
Associate Editorial Director:
 Wanda Nowakowska
Editorial Assistance: Imoinda Romain
Art Director: Gordon Sibley
Graphic Designer: Jennifer Lum
Production Director: Susan Barrable
Production Manager: Sandra L. Hall
Printing and Binding: Tien Wah Press

On Juno Beach
was produced by
Madison Press Books,
which is under the direction of
Albert E. Cummings.

First published in Canada by
Scholastic Canada Ltd.
175 Hillmount Road
Markham, Ontario L6C 1Z7

Printed in Singapore